GREAT TRUTHS OF THE BIBLE

Great Truths of the Bible

PHIL COULSON

40 Beansburn, Kilmarnock, Scotland

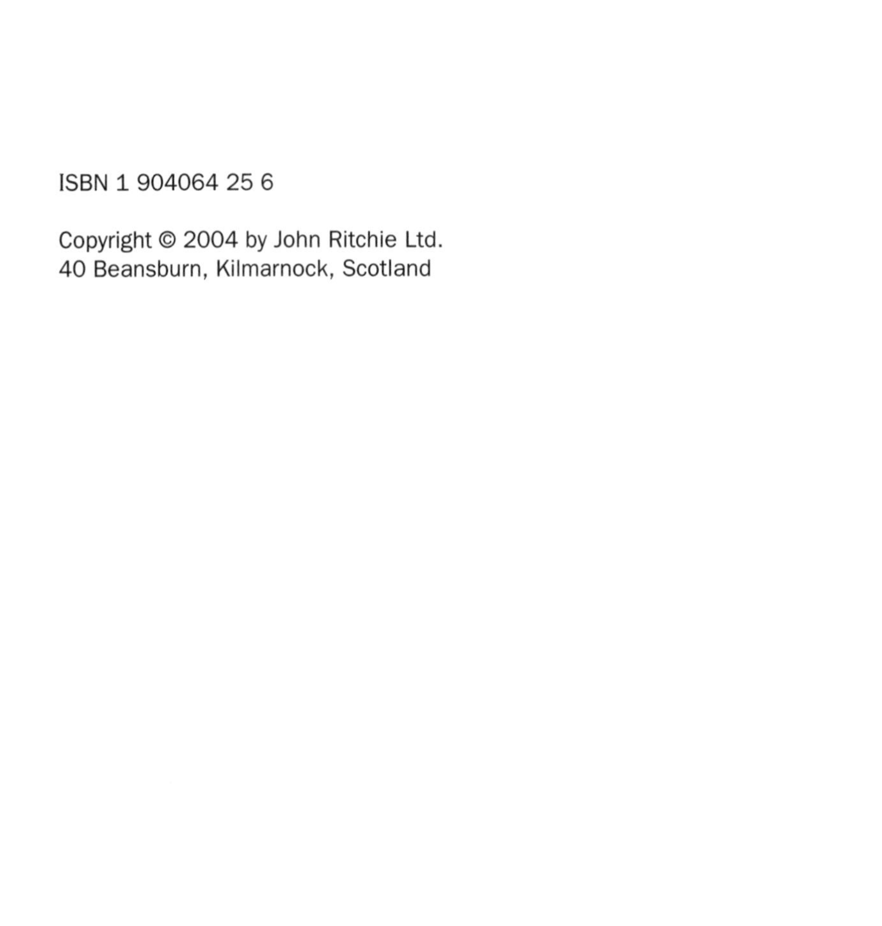

ISBN 1 904064 25 6

40 Beansburn, Kilmarnock, Scotland

Typeset by John Ritchie Ltd., Kilmarnock

Contents

Redemption

Introduction

Every discipline in secular life has its own vocabulary and definitions which must be mastered by those who would excel in that particular calling. This fact is of much greater importance in relation to the Scriptures, because the choice and meaning of its words are not the outcome of human invention, but are those which the Holy Spirit has seen fit to use. How often we sing of "pardon" for sinners, yet the New Testament Scriptures never mention the word because "pardon" is not the same as "justification". The misunderstanding and consequent misuse of scriptural words may lead to confusion and even result in wrong doctrine. Our purpose in this series, God willing, is to examine some of the great truths which are summed up in particular words, with a view to a greater understanding of the terminology of our calling by grace.

The Foundation of Redemption – Purchase

What is redemption?

One of the first points to be understood concerning redemption is that it is not simply the payment of a purchase price in order to obtain someone or something. The Greek word *exagorazo*, which literally means "to buy out", is translated "redeem" in our Bibles and carries the familiar notion of a slave being purchased out of the market with a view to his liberty.

The distinction between ransom and redemption

There is, however, an important distinction between the payment made and the ultimate deliverance of the slave out of bondage. The scriptural word for the payment that makes deliverance possible is "ransom", and, whilst the ransom lays the legal basis for the deliverance of the slave, he does not know the real truth of redemption until he is walking as a free man. Payment establishes legal entitlement to the property and is an essential element of redemption, but the object or person that has been purchased is only redeemed when the legal owner claims the possession for himself, thus providing deliverance from all previous claims. The purchase price secures the possession *for* himself, but deliverance secures the possession *to* himself. Thus redemption is *based upon* the payment of a ransom, but does not *mean* payment or purchase.

Examples of ransom and redemption

The distinction between ransom and redemption is made in Jeremiah 31.11 - "For the Lord hath redeemed Jacob, and ransomed him from the hand of him that was stronger than he". Again, in Hosea 13.14, we read, "I will ransom them from the power of the grave; I will redeem them from death". Noting the distinction between the ransom, which establishes ownership by payment, and redemption which displays ownership by possession, gives help in understanding Ephesians 1.14 - "Which is the earnest of our inheritance until the redemption of the purchased possession". The act of purchase, at Calvary, was at least 2000 years prior to the Lord claiming to Himself that which He has bought with His blood, but, when He does call us all home to glory, that will be the redemption of the purchased possession. One of the clearest illustrations of this aspect of redemption is seen in Jeremiah's experience of buying the field of Hanameel, his cousin, as recorded in Jeremiah 32. Payment of an agreed price was the basis of the redemption of the field, so seventeen shekels of silver were duly paid over and the transaction was witnessed and sealed. The curious nature of the divine instruction to buy the field, as far as Jeremiah was concerned, was that God had already revealed that the whole land, including the newly-bought field, was to be overrun by the Chaldeans. To buy land that was soon to be invaded seemed folly indeed! Jeremiah realised by faith, however, that God was able to deliver the purchased possession, even though many years and the wrongful occupation of the Chaldeans might separate the ransom payment and the final redemption of the field. Legal entitlement had been established, sealed and witnessed, and the passage of time could not erode the authority of the purchaser to claim, one day, that which was lawfully his. We thus observe that payment is with a view to redemption, and establishes legal ownership. Again, by differentiating between the payment made and the deliverance wrought, any previous difficulty in understanding 2 Peter 2.1 should disappear. The false teachers mentioned in that verse, "even denying the Lord that bought them", are included in the purchase price paid in blood at Calvary, but refuse to accept the liberty that has been obtained for them. They are purchased but not redeemed.

The ransom paid by the Lord Jesus

In like manner, "the man Christ Jesus...gave himself a ransom for all" (1 Tim 2.5,6) but not all will thus be saved. So enormous was the price He paid in the giving of Himself, He has obtained the legal right to all things in Heaven and Earth, an illustration of which is seen in Matthew 13.44 where the man sold all that he had to buy the field in which the treasure was hidden. He bought the *whole field* for the sake of the treasure it contained. Interestingly, the Scriptures do not tell us to whom the ransom was paid, and it serves no edifying purpose to speculate, save to say that the payment of a ransom expresses the thought of a costly transaction, implicitly stating the preciousness to the redeemer of the purchased possession.

The Fulfilment of Redemption – Power

The act of redemption

From what we have considered so far, we understand that redemption *as a process* includes the payment of a ransom, but the act of redemption itself is to take into personal possession that which legally belongs to the redeemer. Often in Scripture that act is opposed, so legal entitlement is enforced by strength and power. Nowhere is this more clearly seen than in the redemption from Egypt's bondage of the children of Israel.

Israel redeemed from Egypt

The first recorded song in Scripture is all about the greatness of God in redemption, and in that song we learn of God's wonderful purpose in the redemption of His people: "Thou in thy mercy hast led forth the people which thou hast redeemed: thou hast guided them in thy strength unto thy holy habitation" (Ex 15.13). Was this redemption based upon payment? It was, for in that song on the farther shore of the Red Sea Israel sang of "the people...which thou hast purchased" (Ex 15.16). Here is another indication that literal payment is not always in view, for the children of Israel were already the legal possession of their God by virtue of His sovereign elective will. Nevertheless, Psalm 74.2 says, "Remember thy congregation, which thou hast purchased of old", indicating that a great value and a preciousness are attached to the people of God in His eyes. The redemption of Israel by the strength of the Lord was preceded, of course, by the Passover in Egypt, in which was prefigured the death of Christ and the ransom price that He would pay at Calvary.

"Redeemer" in the NT

Though it is clear that the Lord Jesus paid the ransom upon which the whole work of redemption is based, we do not read of Him as the "Redeemer". In fact, the word "Redeemer" is not mentioned at all in the NT, although it should perhaps be used in Acts 7.35 where the word "deliverer", referring to Moses, is the English translation of the Greek word *lutrotes*. Where *lutrotes* is used in the Septuagint (the Greek version of the OT Scriptures) it is translated "kinsman" in Ruth 3.9, "avenger" in Numbers 35.12, as well as "redeemer" in numerous other references. Thus the same Greek word gives us *redeemer, kinsman, avenger* and *deliverer*. Consider these words in the light of Hebrews 2.14-15: "Forasmuch then as the children are partakers of flesh and blood, he also himself likewise took part of the same (the Kinsman); that through death he might destroy him that had the power of death, that is, the devil (the Avenger); And deliver them who through fear of death were all their lifetime subject to bondage (the Deliverer)". The thought of the Kinsman and the Deliverer in these verses will be readily understood, but an explanation of the Avenger might be in order. In Numbers 35.19 we read "The revenger of blood himself shall slay the murderer: when he meeteth him, he shall slay him". (The *revenger of blood* is the same person as the *avenger* in v.12). In John 8.44 the Lord says of the devil, "He was a murderer from the beginning", and, when He died at Calvary, the divine Avenger "met the murderer and slew him". Payment and power combined at the Cross to provide redemption, and the scriptural summary is this: "By his own blood he entered in once into the holy place, having obtained eternal redemption" (Heb 9.12).

Justification

"For there is no difference: For all have sinned, and come short of the glory of God; Being justified freely by his grace through the redemption that is in Christ Jesus" (Rom 3.22-24).

This quotation from the Roman epistle establishes the link between our consideration last month of Redemption, and the study now of the great truth of Justification. "The redemption that is in Christ Jesus" encompasses the entire work of the Lord Jesus at Calvary, not only in what He did at that time in Earth's history, but also all the divine counsel and purpose that devised, planned, executed and will ultimately bring to completion the wonderful demonstration of God's love to us in Christ. This manifestation of the character of God is the means by which God can justify freely by his grace those who have sinned and come short of the glory of God. "The redemption that is in Christ Jesus" has satisfied every requirement of divine holiness, and provided the channel through which divine grace can flow out to sinners, thus allowing God to "declare...at this time his righteousness: that he might be just, and the justifier of him that believeth in Jesus" (Rom 3.26). Justification, therefore, is an outcome of the redemptive work of the Lord Jesus, and is bestowed freely (without cause) by the grace of God upon sinners who exercise faith in the Lord Jesus Christ. But what does it mean to be justified?

The Meaning of Justification

To "justify" is to clear of every charge and, thus, to account righteous. Immediately we note an important distinction between justification and a word that is not used in the NT Scriptures - "pardon". The person who receives pardon for sins is still guilty, but has been relieved of bearing the judicial consequences of them. The penalty is lifted but the guilt remains. Justification is a higher truth altogether, because those who are justified stand before a holy God as though they had never sinned at all. The question of punishment does not arise because, not only is there no guilt established, but none can bring any accusation. So completely does God justify believers that He challenges the whole universe to lay a charge against them (Rom 8.33). Forgiveness of sins is a wonderful thing, but to be justified is more precious still. That distinction is brought out in Acts 13.38-39: "Through this man is preached unto you the forgiveness of sins: And by him all that believe are justified from all things, from which ye could not be justified by the law of Moses". Well might we sing,

"I hear the accuser roar
Of ills that I have done;
I know them well, and thousands more;
Jehovah findeth none!"

Justified by Grace – The Source of Justification

Justification stems from the grace of God, His totally unmerited, gratuitous kindness towards undeserving, rebellious sinners. It is that essential element of His plan of redemption which desires for sinners that they not only be delivered from eternal punishment (for which the forgiveness of sins would suffice), but that they should also be made acceptable in His presence, able to stand before Him as a holy people. "Being justified freely by his grace" (Rom 3.24) tells us that justification is causeless, in the sense that there is nothing within us or about us to prompt such an act on God's part. It comes in response to nothing other than the overtures of His own grace and boundless love. Hence we read in Romans 5.8, "But God commendeth his (own) love toward us, in that, while we were yet sinners, Christ died for us". The source of justification, therefore, is the heart of God Himself, and His desire in grace that sinners be able to stand in His presence without a stain on their character. However, the means whereby He justifies the sinner must be in keeping with His own holy character.

Justified by Blood – The Basis of Justification

In Romans chs. 1-3 God sits as Judge with the world of men arraigned before Him. Here is the indictment: "All have sinned, and come short of the glory of God"(3.23). Nature, conscience and law all bear their witness, and the inescapable verdict is "Guilty". Every mouth is stopped and the whole world stands guilty before a holy God who, in righteousness, passes down the only possible sentence – "Death". How awesome! How terrible! How final! Not one of us can deny our guilt, or undo our past, or atone in any way for our sins. None of our fellow men can help for they are in the same strait, and the situation is utterly hopeless. This is where the glorious Gospel of the grace of God meets us, and, with inexpressible relief, we hear the divine solution stated: "While we were yet sinners, Christ died for us". Immediately after this we read, "being now justified by his blood"(Rom 5.9), so, if "justification by grace" tells us of the source, "justification by blood" tells us of the means by which the desire of the divine heart is realised in practice. The death of Christ reconciled the desires of divine grace with the demands of divine holiness, and provided a righteous basis upon which God could move out in mercy towards penitent sinners.

It is essential that two main problems are resolved for justification of a condemned sinner to be possible. First, the question of his *sins* must be addressed if he is to escape the judgment he deserves and, second, the question of his *sin* (or *sinnership*) must be dealt with if he is to be reconciled to a holy God. These two requirements are met, typically, in the trespass and sin offerings. The trespass offering dealt with what a man had done, but the sin offering dealt with what he was. This distinction is made doctrinally in the letter to the Romans which teaches us that the death of Christ in the place of the believer deals with what he has done, and the believer's death in Christ deals with what he is by nature. Justification rests upon these twin truths concerning the death of Christ – His death for me saves me from the penalty of my sins, and my death in Him saves me from the power of sin as a master. When Christ died, the believer died, thus satisfying the demands of an inflexible law which, in condemning us, was powerless to help and could only demand death. Our judicial death with Christ has freed us from law's demands and made us the subjects of justification by grace. Every divine requirement was fulfilled in the life and death of the Lord Jesus, and His precious blood is the foundation upon which our justification rests.

Justified by Faith – The Obtaining of Justification

"Therefore being justified by faith, we have peace with God through our Lord Jesus Christ" (Rom 5.1). If divine grace is the source of justification, and the precious blood of Christ the basis of it, then faith is the means by which justification is appropriated by sinners in all their desperate need. The principle of justification by faith is one which knows no dispensational barrier or change, that is, it holds true in every age and for all time. Which of us has not been thrilled to read the eleventh chapter of Hebrews, and to contemplate the great variety of ways in which men and women demonstrated their faith in God? Each of them was the recipient of some revelation of God's holy character and His claims upon them, and each responded by taking God's side in the matter, believing Him and what He had promised, and each was justified by faith. The exercise of faith is contrary to the inclination of the natural mind. The natural mind will consider the circumstances, the visible evidences, the clear pros and cons of any given situation, and come to a conclusion based on reason, sense and a knowledge of the operation of physical laws. When the Old Testament worthies named in Hebrews 11 exercised faith in their own unique situations, it was not that they simply discounted or ignored the apparent impossibility of what God was saying to them. Indeed, Romans 4 makes it clear that Abraham, when told by God that he and Sarah would have a son, did weigh up the apparent impossibility of what God promised. "And being not weak in faith, he considered not his own body now dead, when he was about an hundred years old, neither yet the deadness of Sara's womb: he staggered not at the promise of God through unbelief; but was strong in faith, giving glory to God; and being fully persuaded that, what he had promised, he was able also to perform. And therefore it was imputed to him for righteousness" (Rom 4.19-22). Abraham weighed up the situation in the light of his knowledge of physical things, realised that what God had promised was physically impossible, and then he deliberately set aside the problems in the light of his knowledge of God and simply took God at His word. His act of faith was in weighing up the clear physical impossibilities against the revealed promise of God, and deliberately taking God's side in the matter. His faith was not in the promise but in the God who had made the promise and, "(staggering) not at the promise of God through unbelief", he gave glory to God through his obedience of faith.

The revelation of God's holy claims against sinful men today is by means of "the gospel of God...concerning his Son Jesus Christ our Lord" (Rom 1.1,3). When a sinner understands, by divine illumination, the claims of the gospel, and by deliberate decision takes God at His word concerning his lost condition and the salvation that is to be found in the Lord Jesus, he is exercising the faith that acknowledges that what God has promised He is able also to perform. "And therefore it was imputed to him for righteousness". We should note here that it is the *act* of faith, and not the *amount* of faith, that is important. So often the Adversary attacks us by causing us to doubt if we really did enough when we trusted the Lord for salvation. Did I believe *enough*? Did I say *enough*? Did I understand *enough*? Was I contrite *enough*? Praise God that the sufficiency of our salvation rests in Christ and His atoning work, not in anything that we have or could ever do. The question of "enough" is settled in the sufficiency of Christ, and we need only ask, "Has there been a time when I believed the gospel, repented of my sins and by faith trusted Christ as my Saviour and Lord?" If so, then thank God again right now for saving your soul and for the knowledge that, "being justified by faith, we have peace with God through our Lord Jesus Christ".

Justified by Works – The Evidence of Justification

"Ye see then how that by works a man is justified, and not by faith only" (Jas 2.24). Is this verse at variance with the teaching of the Roman Epistle? No, of course not. The justification that James is speaking of is not justification before God but before men. He is stating that a profession of faith in Christ is substantiated by a change in life. If a person claims to have been justified by faith yet the appetites, associations and activities remain essentially unchanged, then the reality of the profession must be suspect. Our fellow men cannot read our hearts or see our faith, but they can read our lives and observe our walk. Good works and a godly life flow from, and owe their value to, a genuine faith within. The grace that saves a sinner also teaches him "that, denying ungodliness and worldly lusts, we should live soberly, righteously, and godly, in this present world" (Titus 2.12). Such practical righteousness is expected in the lives of all those who bear the Name of Christ, especially in days of easy profession. The only satisfactory proof that we are justified before God by faith is a life of practical righteousness before men, characterised by those "good works, which God hath before ordained that we should walk in them" (Eph 2.10).

Sanctification

The accuracy of a definition of any particular word can be tested by substituting it for the word in question, and ensuring that the sense of the passage is not only retained but, ideally, is made more plain. After much thought, and the application of such a test, the following definition of *sanctify* is offered: *"To set apart from the rest so as to highlight a uniqueness of character that expresses divine purpose"*. However, one might still reasonably question why the usual definition - *to set apart* - is thought inaccurate, and the reason is not so much to do with inaccuracy as with incompleteness. Something might be set apart because its value qualifies it for special attention, or it might be set apart because it is worthless and of no use to its owner. The scriptural sense of sanctification always carries with it the idea of selection for higher service, hence the suggested definition which links the act of setting apart to the intention of the divine mind and will. The reader is invited to test the definition in each mention of the word "sanctify" (and its derivatives) in the Bible, and see if it is valid or not.

As a quick reference, however, consider the following quotations from the book of Exodus: "Sanctify unto me all the firstborn..." (13.2); "And the Lord said unto Moses, Go unto the people, and sanctify them..." (19.10); "I will sanctify also both Aaron and his sons, to minister to me in the priest's office" (29.44). Now, if sanctification merely meant setting something apart to one side, who would have been left of the children of Israel once "all the firstborn", "the people" and "Aaron and his sons" had been set apart? Nobody, of course, because all of the congregation would simply have been moved from one place to another. But if we apply the thought of each act of sanctification expressing a different aspect of divine purpose, then we can see how each of these groups among the children of Israel could be sanctified without the act of setting apart being meaningless.

Besides the references already quoted, it will be found that numerous objects and persons were sanctified in the OT Scriptures, and, in each case, a different aspect of the divine purpose was in view. Mount Sinai was sanctified in Exodus 19.23, and the brazen altar in Exodus 29.36. The laver and its foot were the subject of sanctification in Exodus 40.11, and so the list could go on. Different people and different objects were sanctified at different times, in different ways and for different reasons, and thus tremendous variety marked God's commands to set certain things apart so as to highlight some uniqueness of character that expressed divine purpose. In this way His people were instructed, and, as Hebrews 1.1 teaches us that "God, who at sundry times and in divers manners spake in time past unto the fathers by the prophets", so He also spoke to His people through the truth of sanctification in all its variety.

Before we look at sanctification in relation to the believer, we should note that in every reference to sanctification there is a need to identify (1) the sanctifier; (2) the person or object that is sanctified; and (3) the purpose for which sanctification is effected. For example, in the first reference to sanctification in our Bibles we read, "And God blessed the seventh day, and sanctified it: because that in it he had rested from all his work which God created and made" (Gen 2.3). The Sanctifier is God; the object that is sanctified is the seventh day; the purpose for which it was sanctified was to teach the principle of Sabbath rest, because it was the day in which God Himself had rested. The seventh day was thus set apart from the rest of the days of the week so as to highlight a uniqueness of character that expresses divine purpose.

Sanctification in Relation to the Believer's Salvation

"Peter, an apostle of Jesus Christ, to the strangers scattered throughout Pontus, Galatia, Cappadocia, Asia, and Bithynia, Elect according to the foreknowledge of God the Father, through sanctification of the Spirit, unto obedience and sprinkling of the blood of Jesus Christ: Grace unto you, and peace, be multiplied" (1 Pet 1.1-2). In these opening verses of Peter's first letter, each of the three Persons of the triune Godhead is stated to have an active part in the sovereign purpose of God. The order is the same as that seen in the Creation, namely: the Father is seen as the Architect, "For thus saith the Lord (Jehovah) that created the heavens; God himself that formed the earth and made it; he hath established it, he created it not in vain, he formed it to be inhabited: I am the Lord; and there is none else" (Is 45.18); the Son is seen as the Executor of the divine purpose, "For by him were all things created, that are in heaven, and that are in earth, visible and invisible, whether they be thrones, or dominions, or principalities, or powers: all things were created by him, and for him" (Col 1.16); and the Holy Spirit is seen as the Energiser of that which had been brought into being, "And the Spirit of God moved upon the face of the waters" (Gen 1.2).

So, in the work of salvation that effects a new creation, the Father is the Architect, "Elect according to the foreknowledge of God the Father"; the Son is the Executor of the divine purpose, "(the) sprinkling of the blood of Jesus Christ" (the sprinkling being the seal of obedience as taught in Exodus 24.5-8); and the Holy Spirit is the divine Energiser who illuminates the darkened mind through the application of the word of God, sets apart those who are sovereignly chosen of the Father with a view to obedience, and imparts new life unto those who exercise the obedience of faith. Thus we know "sanctification of the Spirit, unto obedience".

Do not let it be supposed for a moment that the responsibility of the sinner to believe the Gospel is being in any way diminished. It is simply not the principal thought in 1 Peter 1 which is emphasising the glorious sovereignty of our God in the salvation of souls. The same can be said of 2 Thessalonians 2.13, "But we are bound to give thanks alway to God for you, brethren beloved of the Lord, because God hath from the beginning chosen you to salvation through sanctification of the Spirit and belief of the truth". Here again, the way in which the divine purpose is realised in the experience of believers is "through sanctification of the Spirit and belief of the truth". The Holy Spirit is the Sanctifier, those sanctified are men whom God has sovereignly elected to be saved, and the purpose of the sanctification is "belief of the truth". Don't let us be frightened or argumentative about this wonderful aspect of our salvation, neither let us rob God of the glory of His sovereignty in all things, including the salvation of souls. Rather, we should bow in worship and bless the Almighty God of Eternity that He should ever regard rebels such as we with a heart of love and grace, and send His beloved Son into the world to be the Saviour of sinners.

Whereas the sanctifying work of the Holy Spirit effects the divine purpose in bringing us to salvation, the sanctifying work of the Lord Jesus is that which gives us standing before a righteous God. "But of him (God) are ye in Christ Jesus, who of God is made unto us wisdom, and righteousness, and sanctification, and redemption" (1 Cor 1.30). That is, through our identification with Christ He has become to us the divine means of knowing the mind of God, of standing before God, of being set apart for the glory of God, and ultimately of being bodily in the very presence of God. Believers in the Lord Jesus are thus the subjects of divine counsel and intention, "According as he hath chosen us in him before the foundation of the world" (Eph 1.4), and have been set apart by the co-ordinated work and desire of the triune Godhead so that we, a unique people, might be an eternal expression of wonderful divine purpose. This glorious standing must have, of course, a practical outworking in the lives of believers, and that, God willing, will be our study next month.

We observed last month that many different people and objects in the Bible were sanctified at different times, by different means, for different reasons. However, an act of sanctification always finds its source in the revealed purpose of God, so we might say that all sanctification is of God. An act of sanctification must, therefore, be an inherently good thing because its source is divine and its purpose is for His glory. Sanctification does not make something good, but it is the means by which a person or thing is taken up by the sovereign decree of God and used to demonstrate some aspect of His purpose and His ways. Hence the definition suggested last month for the verb "to sanctify": *To set apart from the rest so as to highlight a uniqueness of character that expresses divine purpose.*

Sanctification in Relation to Standing

The point that sanctification does not impart virtue, or give its object standing in the sight of God, is an important one to understand. As far as believers in the Lord Jesus are concerned, our standing before God is on the ground of justification, not sanctification. The doctrine of the gospel of God is expounded in the first eight chapters of the Roman epistle, and the only references to sanctification in that section are in ch.6 where sanctification (translated "holiness" in the AV) is seen as the product of our righteous standing before God, and not the means of it (Rom 6.19 & 22). Again, the fact that sanctification does not impart virtue is evident from Scriptures concerning the Lord Jesus: "Say ye of him, whom the Father hath sanctified, and sent into the world, Thou blasphemest; because I said, I am the Son of God?" (Jn 10.36). If sanctification 'turns the common into the holy' as is sometimes stated, what dreadful implications there would be in this verse! Nothing was ever wanting in the moral and spiritual standing of the Son of God, so His sanctification by the Father clearly has to do with the divine purpose and not with any regenerative or corrective work.

As a final emphasis of the point that sanctification does not affect one's standing before God, consider the statement in 1 Corinthians 7.14: "For the unbelieving husband is sanctified by the wife, and the unbelieving wife is sanctified by the husband: else were your children unclean; but now are they holy". The context of this verse is the question of whether a believing husband or wife is defiled by continuing to live with an unbelieving spouse after conversion. As a married couple, whether or not they are saved, the two are one flesh. The subsequent salvation of one of the partners does not violate or cancel that creatorial principle and, if it did, the apostle argues, the children of that union would not be legitimate, they would be unclean. But it is self-evident that this is not the case, so if the children are legitimate then so must be the marriage. The passage is not teaching that the unbelieving partner is sanctified *as a result* of the other being saved, but that the unbeliever remains sanctified in relation to the marriage bond *even though* the other now believes. The verse has nothing to do with the unbelieving partner deriving any merit or standing through their association with a believer, but their sanctification is in relation to the divinely instituted marriage bond which is not affected by the welfare of their respective souls. The unbeliever in this verse, therefore, remains set apart (unto the marriage bond) so as to highlight a uniqueness of character (as either husband or wife) that expresses divine purpose (the making one flesh of twain).

Sanctification in Relation to Practice

Whilst sanctification does not affect our standing before God, we have a solemn responsibility to live our lives in the conscious knowledge that we are sanctified. The outcome of understanding the doctrine of sanctification ought to be seen in believers living lives that are holy and distinctive. That lovely, dignified description of every child of God, *saint*, comes from the same root as the word *sanctify*, even as Paul wrote to the Corinthians, "to them that are sanctified in Christ Jesus, called saints, with all that in every place call upon the name of Jesus Christ our Lord, both theirs and ours" (1 Cor 1.2). The religious world has its own saints, those whose saintliness is supposed to grant them standing before God. The true saint, however, is a saint *because of* his or her standing before God, and the indwelling Holy Spirit is the source of all the necessary power and ability to live a life that reflects our standing and our divinely appointed purpose. Paul was about to give solemn corrective ministry to the Corinthian assembly, so he immediately reminded them in his salutation of their high calling and the divine purpose for them. Their ungodly practice did not affect in any way their calling as saints, but it certainly did not reflect the truth and the purpose of their calling. The responsibility for conformity to our calling as saints is ours alone.

Sanctification means Holiness

The Greek word *hagiasmos* appears ten times in our New Testament Scriptures, and is translated by the word *sanctification* in five instances, and by the word *holiness* in the rest. So sanctification means holiness in a literal sense, but the truth of sanctification also means practical holiness in a moral sense. In the midst of a growing trend towards the notion that if we conform to the world in its dress, entertainment, speech and social habits we shall be better able to witness to them about the Lord, it is timely to restate, unequivocally, that a holy life is a mandatory requirement of every believer in the Lord Jesus. There are things which are obviously incompatible with those who are 'called saints', as Paul wrote to the Ephesians: "But fornication, and all uncleanness, or covetousness, let it not be once named among you, as becometh saints; neither filthiness, nor foolish talking, nor jesting, which are not convenient: but rather giving of thanks" (Eph 5.3-4). The necessity for such an exhortation reminds us that the potential for such unbecoming conduct lies in every one of us, even though we have been saved by the grace of God. The old nature will exert all its considerable force to take the believer away from a manner of life that pleases God, and holiness of life will be a constant conflict with the flesh until the Lord comes. How solemn it is that amongst the venal sins mentioned in this exhortation to the Ephesians is that of covetousness, which a lexicon defines simply as "a greedy desire to have more". Sadly, it cannot be said that this feature is unknown amongst the saints of God today, and it is not 'becoming (befitting) saints'. The ungodly, conformity to whose manner of life seems not to worry some who profess to be saints, are "the children of disobedience" upon whom "cometh the wrath of God", and we are expressly enjoined; "Be not ye therefore partakers with them" (Eph 5.6-7).

It has often been noted that particular features of new life were seen in the three people whom the Lord raised from the dead. In relation to Jairus' daughter there was *new appetite*; with the widow of Nain's son there was *new affection*; with Lazarus there was *new activity* (Mk 5.43; Lk 7.15; Jn 11.44). In the book of Leviticus the people of God are three times called unto holiness because their God is holy. In ch. 11.41-45 the call to holiness is in relation to *appetite*; in ch. 19.2-4 the call is in relation to *affection*; in ch. 20.22-26 the call is in relation to *activity*. These calls to practical sanctification are entirely relevant for today: "And ye shall not walk in the manners of the nation, which I cast out before you…I am the Lord your God, which have separated you from other people…And ye shall be holy unto me: for I the Lord am holy, and have severed you from other people, that ye should be mine" (Lev 20.23,24,26). "For this is the will of God, even your sanctification" (1 Thess 4.3).

Consecration

Consecration can mean "Sanctification"

Following on from our consideration last month of the practical aspects of sanctification, we turn our attention to the related subject of consecration. Reference to a dictionary shows that the usual understanding of consecration is "to set something aside for sacred use", and in many instances of the word in Scripture that meaning is true. But in the OT the words "consecrate" and "consecration" are used to translate other Hebrew words which have completely different meanings, two of which are of particular interest. Thus the same English words can have three distinct meanings at least, as comparison of various verses will show.

"And they withstood Uzziah the king, and said unto him, It appertaineth not unto thee, Uzziah, to burn incense unto the Lord, but to the priests the sons of Aaron, that are *consecrated* to burn incense" (2 Chr 26.18). The word used here for "consecrated" is the same as that translated "sanctify" in Exodus 40.10; "And thou shalt anoint the altar of the burnt offering, and all his vessels, and *sanctify* the altar: and it shall be an altar most holy". This particular Hebrew word is translated "sanctify" or "holy" in the overwhelming majority of its hundreds of mentions in the OT, and thus supports the link of consecration with sanctification.

Consecration can mean "Completion"

Consider now these Scriptures in which the words in italics are all the same word in Hebrew: "And thou shalt gird them with girdles, Aaron and his sons, and put the bonnets on them: and the priest's office shall be theirs for a perpetual statute: and thou shalt *consecrate* Aaron and his sons" (Ex 29.9); "And God blessed them, saying, Be fruitful, and multiply, and *fill* the waters in the seas, and let fowl multiply in the earth" (Gen 1.22); "And forty days were *fulfilled* for him; for so are *fulfilled* the days of those which are embalmed" (Gen 50.3); "And in cutting of stones, to *set* them, and in carving of timber, to work in all manner of workmanship" (Ex 31.5). These references unfold a different thought of consecration, one in which the idea of completion is brought before us.

Consecration can mean "Dedication"

Of the Nazarite it is said in Numbers 6.12, "And he shall *consecrate* unto the Lord the days of his *separation*, and shall bring a lamb of the first year for a trespass offering". The same original word is used earlier in the chapter; "All the days of the vow of his *separation* there shall no razor come upon his head: until the days be fulfilled, in the which he *separateth* himself unto the Lord, he shall be holy, and shall let the locks of the hair of his head grow. All the days that he *separateth* himself unto the Lord he shall come at no dead body" (Num 6.5-6). This word is used ten times in relation to the Nazarite in Numbers 6, but only twice is it translated "consecration". (Note that the word "fulfilled" in v.5 is the word we looked at in the previous paragraph).

In seeking to understand the meaning of consecration, therefore, we need to think of each of its distinctive meanings in Scripture. Some of the practical considerations of sanctification were discussed last month, and they are true also of our first rendering of consecration, so now we will consider the implications of consecration in its two other meanings of "completion" and "dedication".

The Consecration of the Priests in Leviticus 8

The book of Leviticus is all about access into the presence of God, and that access is based upon the principles taught in the offerings of chs. 1-7. But the offerings required a priesthood to minister at the altar, and the preparation of Aaron and his sons for that work is the subject of Leviticus 8. The consecration of the priests to divine service did not make them priests – they were that by birth and divine calling (Ex 28.1) – but it enabled and authorised them to function as priests in the sanctuary. The details of how the priests were washed and dressed are highly instructive, but are not the subject of this study. Suffice to say that by the end of Leviticus 8.21 the priests are identified, ceremonially clean, dressed appropriately for service and standing in the good of their association with the sin and the burnt offerings. Aaron and his sons stand with all the appearance and authority of priesthood, but until the ram of consecration is offered they still cannot function in the priest's office. Thus the ram of consecration is going to "fill them" for their ministry.

"And (Moses) brought the other ram, the ram of consecration: and Aaron and his sons laid their hands upon the head of the ram. And he slew it; and Moses took of the blood of it, and put it upon the tip of Aaron's right ear, and upon the thumb of his right hand, and upon the great toe of his right foot. And he brought Aaron's sons, and Moses put of the blood upon the tip of their right ear, and upon the thumbs of their right hands, and upon the great toes of their right feet: and Moses sprinkled the blood upon the altar round about" (Lev 8.22-24).

Identification with Aaron the High Priest

The blood of the ram of consecration did certain things for the priests to whom it was applied. The first was to identify them with Aaron the high priest, because what was done to him was also done to them. He has so far been distinctive in his position, his anointing and his dress, but now the priests over whom he is head are linked with him by blood. They were associated with him in the sin offering (v.14) and in the burnt offering (v.18), but now they are identified with him as a person as they are about to put their priesthood into practice. (It is important to note that whenever Aaron or any other priest is spoken of as distinct from all the other priests, as in Leviticus 8.12 for example, he is a type of Christ in His unique ministry. Where his sons are spoken of, apart from him, as in v.13, they are typical of the church in its priestly character. Where Aaron and his sons are spoken of together, as in v.18, the picture is of the church in relation to Christ their High Priest. Noting this distinction will be of help in the study of all the levitical types). We are those priests to whom the blood of the Antitype of the ram of consecration has been applied, and the same blood that cleansed us from our sins has made us fit for the presence of God by linking us not only with the sacrificial work of Christ but also with His glorious Person. Its application to the tip of the right ear, the thumb of the right hand and the great toe of the right foot of Aaron speaks of how the life sacrificed to God was marked by obedience to His will, strength in His service and holiness in a walk that was all for His glory. The same blood, now applied to the priests, speaks of the tremendous responsibility we bear to display the character of our High Priest as we engage in divine service. The anointing oil that was later sprinkled on the priests (v.30) speaks of the ministry of the Holy

Spirit, and the oil and the blood together give us, as priests, discernment as to divine will, strength for divine service and power for a walk in an alien environment which will all bring glory to our God.

Identification with the Altar

As well as identifying the priests with their High Priest, the blood of the ram of consecration also linked those priests forever with the altar of sacrifice (v.24). Their ministry would always be in the light of the necessity of the brazen altar, and it was intended that as they moved in service for God the fire and the smoke and the blood of the altar would so impress them that their fear of God and their awareness of the dignity attached to His service would be very real indeed. God grant us, as holy and royal priests, a true understanding of these things!

Consecration – the secret of separation

We have already seen that consecration can be viewed from at least three particular angles, the first being to set apart for sacred use. That thought, allied to the similar principle of sanctification, is one we are familiar with and it is illustrated in 2 Chronicles 26.18, "And they withstood Uzziah the king, and said unto him, It appertaineth not unto thee, Uzziah, to burn incense unto the Lord, but to the priests the sons of Aaron, that are *consecrated* to burn incense".

The second meaning of consecration is that of fulfilment, or completion to fulfil a work, and that is illustrated in Exodus 29.9, "And thou shalt gird them with girdles, Aaron and his sons, and put the bonnets on them: and the priest's office shall be theirs for a perpetual statute: and thou shalt *consecrate* Aaron and his sons". We looked at this aspect of consecration in some detail last month, so now we need to think of the third distinct use of the word which concerns dedication to God and the willing commitment of resources to Him. Before we do that, however, let's share a practical thought from our consideration last month of the consecration of the priesthood.

The external coverings of the tabernacle were made of badgers' skins and rams' skins dyed red (Ex 26.14), the rams' skins forming the inner cover of the two. The strong and impervious badger skin is spoken of only in connection with the tabernacle and the shoes which God gave, metaphorically, to Israel in Ezekiel 16.10. As the badgers' skins formed the barrier between the outside world and the sacred things of the tabernacle, and, in Ezekiel 16.10, formed the barrier between the foot of the Israelite and the sands of the desert, so there is the need for that impervious barrier between the believer and the things of the world.

That much is true, but we must not forget that there were two coverings, not one, for the tabernacle. Underlying the badgers' skins was a covering made of rams' skins dyed red, and those rams' skins take us back to the thought of the ram of consecration. The practical thought is this. When we seek to teach the principle of separation from the world and its ways, particularly to younger believers, we should remember that underlying the truth of separation is the truth of consecration. Rather than simply impress on believers the things which they ought not to be involved with, we should positively give them things to "fill the hand". If separation, seen in the badgers' skins, is about denial and refusal to be associated with the things of the world, then consecration, depicted by the rams' skins, is about occupation with the things of the Lord and having the spiritual hands full of things concerning Himself.

Those of us who have reared children will know that if the child has hold of something which could be harmful to it, there are three possible courses of action. The first is to ignore the problem, and that would be irresponsible and unthinkable. The second is to snatch away the offending article, leaving the young one safer but confused and upset. The third course of action is to offer something wholesome to the child who, in reaching out for that which is good, releases that which is potentially injurious. There is much that our young folk may inadvertently have hold of which is potentially injurious to their spiritual health, but ministry on the "badgers' skins" alone may lead to resentment and confusion. We need to remember the underlying truth of consecration, and seek to fill the hands, heads and hearts of these dear believers with things that are spiritually wholesome. The hand that is already full has no capacity left for other things, and the believer who is enjoying the things of the Lord will prove that consecration is the secret of separation. We must be careful that in teaching the necessary truth of separation we do not create a vacuum in which we have taken something away without replacing it with something better. If we are concerned about some of the places to which our youngsters go, are we making the positive effort to open our own homes to them so that they can come and enjoy spiritual things in a godly environment? If the leisure activities of the young ones are a concern, are we prepared to devote our own time to their spiritual wellbeing, always remembering that they *are* young and need to relax, have fun together and enjoy their youth? May the Lord help those of us who are older to so encourage and care for the younger believers that their separation from undesirable things is the outcome of an occupation with the wholesome things which we have taken care to provide.

Consecration – the secret of a distinctive walk

So far we have thought about consecration being the secret of separation from ungodly things, but the third particular use of the word brings out a more positive aspect of separation. In the law of the Nazarite taught in Numbers 6 the words *separation* and *consecration* are used interchangeably, but the emphasis is always upon separation *unto* rather than separation *from*. "And the Lord spake unto Moses, saying, Speak unto the children of Israel, and say unto them, When either man or woman shall separate themselves to vow a vow of a Nazarite, to separate themselves unto the Lord: He shall separate himself from wine and strong drink, and shall drink no vinegar of wine, or vinegar of strong drink, neither shall he drink any liquor of grapes, nor eat moist grapes, or dried. All the days of his separation shall he eat nothing that is made of the vine tree, from the kernels even to the husk. All the days of the vow of his separation there shall no razor come upon his head: until the days be fulfilled, in the which he separateth himself unto the Lord, he shall be holy, and shall let the locks of the hair of his head grow. All the days that he separateth himself unto the Lord he shall come at no dead body. He shall not make himself unclean for his father, or for his mother, for his brother, or for his sister, when they die: because the consecration of his God is upon his head. All the days of his separation he is holy unto the Lord" (Num 6.1-8). In these verses the paramount thought for the Nazarite was that he or she was separated "unto the Lord". It was not that the Nazarite was set apart for holy service, as is the first meaning of consecration that we considered, nor yet that the Nazarite was rendered complete for holy service, as we discussed in the second meaning of the word. Rather it was that the Nazarite took the singular step of absolute devotion to God Himself, to be the object of His pleasure alone. This act of consecration brought with it a mandatory distinctiveness in appetite (Num 6.3-4), appearance (6.5) and associations (6.6-7). “All the days of his separation (consecration) he is holy (sanctified) unto the Lord” (6.8). So many of us are afraid today of being distinctive in our ways, of truly walking as a holy people in the midst of an ungodly and corrupt environment. Does this tell us something of the degree of commitment and devotion we are prepared to make to our God? We are ready to devote time and self to particular avenues of service for Him, perhaps, but what about our devotion to Him alone whose love, compassion, mercy and grace we have all received?

What a lovely example of this whole-hearted devotion is seen in Mary of Bethany whose love for the Lord and occupation with Him made her count so lightly the things that others thought important. She cared not for the misunderstanding of those around, nor did she hoard her material wealth. She was content to lay her all at the feet of the Saviour and, having anointed Him, to then use the God-given glory of her hair to wipe those feet. Is this not consecration in the ultimate? Does she not teach us the blessedness of each of the three main meanings of consecration? Separated unto His service, her heart filled with His glories, she laid herself and all that she had at His feet in absolute devotion. “And who then is willing to consecrate his service this day unto the Lord?” (1 Chr 29.5).

Propitiation

The word *propitiation* occurs just three times in the Authorised Version of the Bible, yet it is, arguably, the keystone of the doctrine of the Gospel of God concerning His Son, Jesus Christ our Lord. Without propitiation there could be no atonement, redemption or justification, and helpless sinners would forever perish under the unmitigated and wholly righteous judgment of God. If the whole work of redemption is a wonderful edifice to the glory of God, then that monument to His grace stands eternally upon the principle of propitiation.

The Significance of Propitiation

A suggested definition of the biblical use of *propitiation* is, "the means by which the wrath of an offended God is appeased in such a way as to prevent the otherwise inevitable visitation of judgment upon the fallen race of men". The righteousness of God demands the administration of summary punishment for sin and, without any intervention, that punishment must be immediate and final. God does not, and cannot, either overlook sin or simply postpone judgment for it in the way that we might perhaps put off the correction of a disobedient child. Every divine act must be consistent with the demands of a righteousness which is not according to some Self-designed code or law but which is the very nature of God Himself. Were it not for propitiation, sinners would be unreachable by divine grace and eternally estranged from the love that desires their salvation. How vital, then, is this great truth! It is nothing less than the establishment of a foundation upon which God can demonstrate, without violating His own righteous demands, His love and mercy to a rebellious race which He sees wallowing in the indescribably offensive filth of its own sin. But how can such propitiation be made?

The Source of Propitiation – 1 John 4.10

The hymnwriter summed up the situation well in the words, "How helpless, how hopeless we sinners had been, if He never had loved us till cleansed from our sin!". Not only was the fallen race of men totally bereft, spiritually and morally, of any acceptable offering to effect propitiation, it was so careless of its condition before God that it engaged in open hostility, rebellion and defiance against Him. Clearly no propitiation would or could ever come from mankind, so whence came it?

"Herein is love, not that we loved God, but that he loved us, and sent his Son to be the propitiation for our sins" (1 Jn 4.10). Here is the wonderful, mighty source of the propitiation that was needed. It emanated from the heart of God, and He provided what He Himself demanded in order that He could righteously express His love toward fallen man. What worship this should provoke in the hearts of men, especially those of us who are saved by God's grace!

The first soul-thrilling assurance we can glean from this verse is that, if God Himself provided the propitiation necessary to satisfy His own righteous demands, the propitiation provided must be completely adequate. He alone knew the requirement, and He alone knew the virtues of the propitiation He sent, so we can rest fully upon the adequacy of the Lord Jesus, the Son of God, as "the propitiation for our sins".

Secondly, the verse teaches us that the Lord Jesus is the propitiation for our sins. John is writing to believers in the Lord Jesus, redeemed by His precious blood, and to this select company he writes of the "propitiation for our sins". Thus the value of the propitiatory work of the Lord Jesus is reckoned to the believer alone and, necessarily, that means the ungodly are outside of the blessed relief from wrath that propitiation has provided for the saints of God.

The Scope of Propitiation – 1 John 2.2

The foregoing sentence might raise the question, "What about the statement in 1 John 2.2 - 'And he is the propitiation for our sins: and not for ours only, but also for the sins of the whole world' - does that not mean a universal propitiation?" A fair question indeed, and one which is raised because of a rare but singularly inappropriate inclusion by the respected translators of the AV. The correct reading of this verse, based on the recognised original texts is: "And he is the propitiation for our sins; but not for ours alone, but also for the whole world". It is important to understand the difference in these two renderings. For the believer, the Lord Jesus is the propitiation for our sins, personally and eternally, and He has satisfied the claims of God in relation to our personal guilt with the outcome that we are forever delivered from divine judgment. But that cannot be said of all men irrespective of their attitude to divine things. John does say that Christ is also the propitiation for the whole world, but he does not say *for the sins of* the whole world. If the AV rendering were correct, then the whole world would be saved, and we know that is not the case. The helpful comment in Vine's Expository Dictionary is, "The italicised addition in the A.V., *"the sins of,"* gives a wrong interpretation. What is indicated is that provision is made for the whole world, so that no one is, by Divine pre-determination, excluded from the scope of God's mercy; the efficacy of the propitiation, however, is made actual for those who believe". The divinely-provided propitiation has made it possible for God to extend mercy to the whole world, withholding judgment while the claims and invitation of the gospel go forth in grace, but the Lord is the propitiation for the sins only of those who believe.

The Sufficiency of Propitiation – Romans 3.25-26

Whereas the two references to propitiation in John's first epistle are the same word in the original, and carry the thought of the Lord being the propitiation for our sins, the word used in Romans 3.25 is used also in Hebrews 9.5 where it is translated *mercyseat*. The purpose of the mercyseat as taught in Exodus 25.22 is, "there I will meet with thee, and I will commune with thee from above the mercy seat, from between the two cherubim which are upon the ark of the testimony". This place of divine communication and fellowship covered the ark and its contents which were the tables of stone, the golden pot of manna, and Aaron's rod that budded. These items testified to Israel's three great sins in the wilderness which are, in principle at least, reviewed in the first two chapters of the Roman epistle. The tables of stone were a reminder of Israel's idolatrous and licentious behaviour when Moses was in the mount, behaviour of the type condemned in Romans 1.18-32. The manna was despised by Israel in the same way as the riches of God's goodness are despised in Romans 2.1-16, and the rod recalls the sin of Korah and his company whose presumptuous ritualism was like that mentioned in Romans 2.17-29.

Just as the mercyseat covered the contents of the ark from the gaze of the downward-looking cherubim (representative of the unswervingly righteous standards of God), so the One whom God has "set forth to be a propitiation" provides the means whereby the three groups of people seen in the first two chapters can have their sins dealt with and put away out of sight. The mercyseat was not the place where expiation for sin was made - that work was all accomplished at the brazen altar - but the blood of the victim was sprinkled on and before the mercyseat to demonstrate that propitiation was complete. Hence the word in this verse is really *mercyseat* or *propitiatory*, emphasising that the One who is set forth has finished the work in relation to the sin question, and, having taken humanity into Heaven, He eternally testifies to His own sufficiency as the propitiation for our sins. This is all by (on the ground of) his blood, and appropriated by faith (v.25).

Finally, these verses state twice that the work of propitiation is a declaration of the righteousness of God and has been accomplished so that God might be just and (yet also) the justifier of him that believeth in Jesus. The ground upon which God can display His unmerited love and mercy to fallen men is nothing less than the glorious person and sacrificial work of His own beloved Son who is the propitiation for our sins.

Predestination

A common misunderstanding about Predestination

Whenever the subject of predestination is mentioned it immediately revives a memory in this writer's mind of an occasion nearly 30 years ago. It was a wet and windy day in the Lake District, and in a "christian" guest house a lively discussion arose on the subject of salvation. Without exception, each of the participants spoke of "predestination" as though it were synonymous with "election" and for that reason, as well as others, the conversation was generally fruitless. The subject of "election" will be dealt with in a later article, God willing, so it will suffice for now to stress that "election" is a truth that concerns sinners before they are saved, and "predestination" applies only to believers in the Lord Jesus Christ once they have been saved. Predestination has nothing whatever to do with unregenerate souls.

The meaning of Predestination

The Greek word *horizo* means *to mark out in a definite way,* or, *to determine the scope of something by setting distinct boundaries*. It is the word from which our English word "horizon" is derived, by which we may immediately think of that distinct line between the sky and the sea that we observe from the beach on a fine day. What that distinct line is doing, however, is marking the limit of our vision, and it is that thought of setting a boundary that is the usual meaning of the word in Scripture. The word is further refined when we consider its contextual use, such as in Acts 17.24-26: "God that made the world and all things therein...hath made of one blood all nations of men for to dwell on all the face of the earth, and hath *determined* (horizo) the times before appointed, and the bounds of their habitation". The scope of the ages has been marked out, and the geographical boundaries within which men are to dwell have been divinely appointed.

In Acts 2.22-23 Peter preaches, " Jesus of Nazareth...being delivered by the *determinate* (horizo) counsel and foreknowledge of God, ye have taken, and by wicked hands have crucified and slain". His preaching accords with the Lord's own words in Luke 22.21-22: "But, behold, the hand of him that betrayeth me is with me on the table. And truly the Son of man goeth, as it was *determined* (horizo): but woe unto that man by whom he is betrayed!". These verses show us that the defining hand of God is active in relation to both creation and redemption, and the bounds and limitations that He appoints are not accidental, arbitrary or capricious but deliberate, co-ordinated limits that are part of an over-arching eternal purpose.

The Greek word translated "predestinate(d)" in the Authorised Version is the word we have just examined, *horizo*, with the prefix *pro* (meaning "before"), thus forming the word *proorizo*. The meaning of predestination, therefore, may be rendered, *the prior determination, in accordance with an over-arching design and purpose, of the scope of a particular work.* In four of the six occasions where the word is used in the NT it is translated "predestinate(d)", the other two mentions being rendered "determined before" (Acts 4.28) and "ordained" (1 Cor 2.7).

Predestination in Romans 8

In the first eight chapters of the epistle to the Romans the apostle Paul, inspired by the Holy Spirit, lays out the doctrine of "the gospel of God...concerning His Son Jesus Christ our Lord" (Rom 1.1-3). He systematically teaches how sins and sin have been dealt with by the death and resurrection of Christ and, at the end of ch.8 he calls upon any contradictory force in the universe to bring a legal challenge against the righteous standing of the child of God. No being in the material or spiritual creation, however great their malignity to God and His glory, can lay anything to the charge of God's elect because the deliverance of guilty souls from the kingdom of darkness has been effected not only by superior power but also by legal redemption. There can be "no separation" at the end of the chapter because there is "no condemnation" at the beginning of it. But immediately before Paul issues the challenge in vv. 31-39 he speaks of the groanings of creation and, likewise, the groanings of individual believers as we await "the redemption of our body" (v.23). In contrast to what we do not know in v.26, he says in vv. 28-30, "And we know that all things work together for good to them that love God, to them who are the called according to his purpose. For whom he did foreknow, he also did predestinate to be conformed to the image of his Son, that he might be the firstborn among many brethren. Moreover whom he did predestinate, them he also called: and whom he called, them he also justified: and whom he justified, them he also glorified".

Those who groan and know not what to pray for are like Job who said, "Behold, I go forward, but he is not there; and backward, but I cannot perceive him: On the left hand, where he doth work, but I cannot behold him: he hideth himself on the right hand, that I cannot see him" (Job 23.8-9). Over these verses we could write, "I know not", but in the very next verse Job says, "But he knoweth the way that I take: when he hath tried me, I shall come forth as gold". Is not this where the child of God finds rest? "I know not...He knows". Every detail and circumstance of life is either ordained or permitted by God according to His purpose, and the believer clings to this knowledge that all things work together for good to them that love God.

But why should God so care for us? Though saved by His grace, what are we to Him? The answer is in the chapter – we have been placed as sons (the literal meaning of "adoption") before Him. To save us He sent His Son (Rom 8.3), the Holy Spirit now witnesses that we are sons (vv.15-16), and the ultimate goal of salvation is conformity to the image of his Son (v.29). This is what God predestinated us to. The word *horizo* could have been used, telling us that God has determined that we should be conformed to the image of His Son, but the Spirit rather used the word *proorizo* to emphasise that all our glorious future by grace was already settled in the most distant possible past. God's purpose is not only to save sinners from condemnation, wonderful though that is, but also to bring them into the moral likeness of His own beloved Son! This is God's objective in the gospel – to populate heaven with billions of redeemed souls who are just like Christ.

Predestination in Ephesians 1

The realisation of the believer's predestination in Romans 8 is still future, but the predestination spoken of in Ephesians 1.3-5 is present. "Blessed be the God and Father of our Lord Jesus Christ, who hath blessed us...Having predestinated us unto the adoption of children by Jesus Christ to himself". "The adoption of children" is literally "the placing of sons", so that we are not only the children of God by new birth but we have also been placed as sons in the family before Him. "The placing of sons" can otherwise be thought of as "sonship", and that status applies to all believers. Sisters in Christ are sons, not daughters, because sonship is not an expression of gender but of relationship to the Father. A true son bears the character of the father (like father, like son), and the present placing as sons will find its completion when full conformity to Christ is realised, as we have seen in Romans 8.

Linked with "sonship" is "heirship", as taught in Galatians 4.7; "Wherefore thou art no more a servant, but a son; and if a son, then an heir of God through Christ". Thus Ephesians 1.11 states; "In whom also we have obtained an inheritance, being predestinated according to the purpose of him who worketh all things after the counsel of his own will".

Predestination is the divine decision to bring redeemed souls into the relationship of sons to a Father, each one conformed to the image of His peerless, pre-eminent Son, and to bestow upon them "an inheritance incorruptible, and undefiled, and that fadeth not away, reserved in heaven for you" (1 Pet 1.4). "Blessed be the God and Father of our Lord Jesus Christ...".

Identification

What is meant by Identification?

The title of this article has been chosen to express an important principle in Scripture. The principle may also be entitled *Representation* because it concerns the deeds of a person or persons in the past being transmitted to people who live long after the historical event. An immediate example will help. In Amos 2.10 God says to His people through the prophet, "Also I brought you up from the land of Egypt, and led you forty years through the wilderness, to possess the land of the Amorite". But the people to whom Amos spoke had never been in Egypt, neither had they known the wilderness journey which took place hundreds of years before. On what basis, then, did God demand that they change their behaviour in the light of these experiences? He held them responsible because they were associated by birth with those who had been in Egypt and the wilderness actually and historically. The Jews of Amos' day were identified with their forefathers' experience.

Identification in Romans 5.12

Association by birth is the principle that underpins the teaching of Romans 5.12. Up to this point in the epistle Paul has explained the truth of justification and stated that God can be just and yet be the justifier of him that believeth in Jesus (Rom 3.26). That justification comes by faith, not works, and "being justified by faith we have peace with God through our Lord Jesus Christ" (Rom 5.1).

In Romans 5.12 Paul turns from the question of sins to the matter of sin itself so that he can show how the finished work of the Lord Jesus, in dealing with this root problem, has enabled the righteous forgiveness of sins. He states, "Wherefore, as by one man sin entered into the world, and death by sin; and so death passed upon all men, for that all have sinned...Therefore as by the offence of one judgment came upon all men to condemnation; even so by the righteousness of one the free gift came upon all men unto justification of life. For as by one man's disobedience many were made sinners, so by the obedience of one shall many be made righteous" (Rom 5.12, 18-19). These verses highlight the difference in the deeds, but the sameness of the principle, between the first and the last Adam. Both Adam and Christ are seen as the head of a family or order of man. Each is said to have committed one outstanding act, Adam's being one of disobedience and Christ's one of obedience. The effects of these outstanding acts are transmitted and reckoned to all who are identified by birth with these historical men. In speaking of Adam's one historical act of disobedience in Eden, the Scripture states that all who are associated with Adam by natural birth are partakers of that one deed and inheritors of Adam's fallen nature. This is the fundamental truth of what constitutes us sinners. Our condition as sinners is not the result of our behaviour but the result of our birth. We stand identified with the fallen head of the human race and the only thing that can break that association is death.

It is a common feature of gospel preaching that the audience is exhorted to accept their condition as sinners by considering various types of wrongdoing. The point might be better made that we are all sinners by reason of our birth and nothing but death will change that. Of course, our sins have to be acknowledged and repented of, and the resulting forgiveness frees us from the penalty of those sins. But our fundamental sinful state needs to be dealt with as well, and it is not forgiveness but death which deals with that. Thus Romans 5 goes on to teach us that, in the same way as we are sinners by association with Adam, so we are righteous by association with Christ.

How do we come into the good of that? By dying to the old order of man headed by Adam, and being born anew into the family headed by our Lord Jesus Christ. Those who are identified with Him by new birth come into all the effects of His outstanding act of obedience, and by wonderful grace they are constituted righteous.

How then do we die to Adam? In the death of Christ. When Christ died, we died - not physically, but unto the old order of man. Here is identification in the ultimate. The Lord Jesus died a literal, physical, agonising death of suffering and shame, and in so doing God "hath made him to be sin for us, who knew no sin; that we might be made the righteousness of God in him" (2 Cor 5.21). That death is reckoned to every believer in the Lord Jesus, and it severs once and for all the link with Adam and the fall. If the death of Christ for me saves me from the penalty of my sins and delivers me from judgment, then my death with Christ is what saves me from the power of sin and delivers me from the dominion of the Devil. Not only that, but I have been raised with Christ so that I am alive unto Him, "For as in Adam all die, even so in Christ shall all be made alive" (1 Cor 15.22). This is what Paul was referring to when he wrote to the Galatians, "I am crucified with Christ: nevertheless I live; yet not I, but Christ liveth in me: and the life which I now live in the flesh I live by the faith of the Son of God, who loved me, and gave himself for me" (Gal 2.20).

Identification in the book of the Acts

Keeping this principle of identification in mind will help immensely in understanding the events recorded in the early chapters of the Acts. Chapter 2 records the occasion of the birth of the Church when the disciples in the upper room were baptised in the Holy Spirit. The disciples were a company of real people in a real room in Jerusalem. They were literally baptised, immersed, in the Holy Spirit: "And when the day of Pentecost was fully come, they were all with one accord in one place. And suddenly there came a sound from heaven as of a rushing mighty wind, and it filled all the house where they were sitting" (Acts 2.1-2). Of this occasion 1 Corinthians 12.13 says, "For by one Spirit are we all baptized into one body", and reference to the original text will show that the preposition would be better translated, "For *in* one Spirit...". That is, although you and I were not in that upper room, and although we live some 2000 years later, we are identified by birth with those who were actually and historically there. The moment we were saved we came into the good of all that those disciples experienced, and understanding this truth is the antidote to so-called Pentecostalism.

As we read further in Acts we find in ch. 8 that the first Samaritans were saved, but, though saved and baptised, they had not yet received the Holy Spirit. Not until Peter and John came down from Jerusalem and laid hands on them did they receive the Holy Spirit. "Ah!", say those who teach that the reception of the Holy Spirit is something that occurs subsequent to salvation and, particularly, baptism, "doesn't this account prove what we say?". Not at all. God was demonstrating that the Church would include Jews, Samaritans and, later, Gentiles, but the Jews had for centuries refused all dealings with the Samaritans (Jn 4.9). Thus the first Samaritans to be saved had to submit to the laying on of Jewish hands, not to impart the Holy Spirit, but to demonstrate that these believers were all one in Christ. The Holy Spirit endorsed that on that one historic occasion. Every Samaritan saved subsequent to that event stands associated with those who were actually there, and a Samaritan saved today would immediately be indwelt by the Holy Spirit.

So, too, with the first Gentiles to be saved, in Acts 10. The bringing into the Church of Cornelius, along with those of his kinsmen and friends who were saved as Peter preached, was accompanied by their speaking with tongues (Acts 10.46). This sign was to give the Jews confidence that God was indeed including Gentiles in the Church. There is no reason for Gentiles to expect to speak with tongues as an evidence of salvation today because they stand identified with those who were actually there in Cornelius' house.

Election

Election unto salvation may offend human reasoning...

For some reason, the subject of our study this month can cause the hackles to rise on the most moderate of men. The heart of the problem lies not in the sublime truth of Election, a doctrine which is straightforward and, in its fundamental concept, not difficult to grasp, but rather in the dilemma which this doctrine poses to the natural mind. In that seat of severely limited capacity to understand the mind and ways of God, we find it impossible to reconcile the idea of sovereign choice with the equally scriptural doctrine of man's individual responsibility to obey the gospel. To human thinking these two principles are diametrically opposed and irreconcilable. Why should it be thought strange that we are incapable of comprehending the infinitude of the divine purpose, and of quantifying in human terms, this expression of God's eternal majesty and glory. Our late beloved brother Mr Jack Hunter would teach individual election from Ephesians 1 and tell us, "Brethren, our minds are too small to grasp the immensity of this truth, but our hearts are big enough to believe it by faith".

Whilst we have spoken of irreconcilable truths, it must be understood, of course, that these two principles need no reconciliation except in the puny domain of human reasoning. They sit in perfect accord in the mind of God, and every attempt to express them to the satisfaction of human logic will certainly fail. If it were possible in any way for the harmony of these two principles to be expressed in words, then surely the Holy Spirit would have done so in the Scriptures. Rather, He has deliberately set the two principles side by side so as to teach us that their ultimate harmony is beyond our present ability to grasp.

...but it is in total harmony with human responsibility

The Lord Jesus said, "All things are delivered unto me of my Father: and no man knoweth the Son, but the Father; neither knoweth any man the Father, save the Son, and he to whomsoever the Son will reveal him" (Mt 11.27). Such a verse makes a clear statement concerning the sovereign, elective will of God in relation to individuals from among the race of men. If the Son does not reveal the Father, He cannot be known. To the unbiased mind this is a crystal-clear declaration of individual election. The very next verse, however, says, "Come unto me, all ye that labour and are heavy laden, and I will give you rest", and thus human responsibility is placed by the Spirit of God immediately alongside the truth of election. The same pattern is seen in John 6.37 where the Lord Jesus says, "All that the Father giveth me shall come to me; *(divine election)* and him that cometh to me I will in no wise cast out *(human responsibility)*. The pattern is seen in practice with Lydia, "whose heart the Lord opened, *(His sovereignty)* that she attended unto the things which were spoken of Paul" *(her responsibility)*. (Acts 16.14). May God grant us grace to acknowledge humbly our smallness and His greatness, and simply accept by faith that the Scriptures teach both truths with equal weight.

In relation to the salvation of the soul, election is always individual...

The Scriptures teach, unequivocally, that God has chosen certain individuals to be saved, and He has done so on the grounds of His own sovereign will in the outworking of His purpose in redemption. We can boldly assert this truth as both scriptural and unassailable. Moreover, it is not a principle that is confined to the gospel, but one that was evident in OT times as well. For example, the inspired words of Paul to the Romans are based upon God's sovereign dealings recorded in Genesis 25.23 and Exodus 33.19: "As it is written, Jacob have I loved, but Esau have I hated. What shall we say then? Is there unrighteousness with God? God forbid. For he saith to Moses, I will have mercy on whom I will have mercy, and I will have compassion on whom I will have compassion. So then it is not of him that willeth, nor of him that runneth, but of God that sheweth mercy" (Rom 9.13-16). Which of us would dare to challenge God's absolute right to bestow blessing upon any individual of His choice? One often hears the complaint, "But it's not fair!", as though the divine will should conform to our concept of what is right. Equally as often, the charge is made that if God chooses certain to be saved He must, of necessity, be consigning others to judgment. That charge might be logical, but it is absolutely unscriptural and wrong. Those who disobey the demands of the gospel consign themselves to judgment, and those who bow in obedience discover the wonderful truth that "he hath chosen us in him before the foundation of the world" (Eph 1.4).

The truth of individual election is emphatically taught in the parenthetic section of the Roman Epistle, chs. 9-11. Indeed, if we fail to see that, we miss the whole point of that part of the doctrine of the gospel. The Jew was resting upon his Scripture-based knowledge of God's sovereign choice of the nation for blessing. As far as the Jew was concerned, God was bound by His word to pour blessing upon them and judgment upon the Gentile. The nation's refusal to see that God's choice of them was not in relation to the salvation of their individual souls provoked the heartfelt cry of the apostle that "my heart's desire and prayer to God for Israel is, that they might be saved" (Rom 10.1). Paul clearly teaches that, in relation to the salvation of the soul, the elective will of a sovereign God is toward individual people.

As well as in Romans and also Ephesians 1, individual election is unequivocally stated in the preaching of Paul and Barnabas in Antioch of Pisidia. "Then Paul and Barnabas waxed bold, and said, It was necessary that the word of God should first have been spoken to you: but seeing ye put it from you, and judge yourselves unworthy of everlasting life *[note the self-consignment to judgment]*, lo, we turn to the Gentiles. For so hath the Lord commanded us, saying, I have set thee to be a light of the Gentiles, that thou shouldest be for salvation unto the ends of the earth. And when the Gentiles heard this, they were glad, and glorified the word of the Lord: and as many as were ordained to eternal life believed" (Acts 13.46-48).

Paul's words to the Thessalonians (2 Thess 2.13) confirm not only their individual election, but also that it was "to salvation". The means by which God brought that purpose to fruition was "through sanctification of the Spirit and belief of the truth" (note well the "balancing" statement of 1 Thess 2.13). Individual election "to eternal life" and "to salvation" is thus a clear scriptural doctrine.

...but there is a corporate aspect in relation to Israel's blessing as a nation

There is no doubt that Israel's appointment to blessing over the other nations of the earth was of a corporate, collective nature. We read, "Behold, the heaven and the heaven of heavens is the Lord's thy God, the earth also, with all that therein is. Only the Lord had a delight in thy fathers to love them, and he chose their seed after them, even you above all people, as it is this day" (Deut 10.14-15). As we have seen, this was the backdrop to Paul's teaching of individual election to salvation (as distinct from merely external privilege) in Romans 9-11. God's statement, "Israel is my son" (Ex 4.22), shows that their election and sonship were collective, but the NT teaches that our election and sonship are individual. Thus there is no scriptural warrant for extending the idea of corporate election to the Church. You and I are not elect because we are in the Church, we are in the Church because we are the elect of God, sovereignly, gloriously, wonderfully chosen by God to be saved by His grace! Should we not humbly and thankfully adopt the attitude of Abraham's servant? "And the man bowed down his head, and worshipped the Lord" (Gen 24.26). Amen.

Glorification

The Nature of Glory

The theme of glory is both wide and extensive in Scripture, so, in this article, the surface of this wonderful subject will only be lightly scratched. The failure of the human mind to appreciate the nature of glory was particularly evident in the days of the Lord's ministry upon earth. The majority of men would say, "Is not this the carpenter, the son of Mary...?" (Mk 6.3). In accordance with Isaiah's prophecy their attitude was "he hath no form nor comeliness; and when we shall see him, there is no beauty that we should desire him" (Is 53.2). Consequently, we read at the end of Mark 6.3, "And they were offended at him". On the other hand, how beautiful is John's testimony; "And the Word was made flesh, and dwelt among us, (and we beheld his glory, the glory as of the only begotten of the Father,) full of grace and truth" (Jn 1.14). An unbelieving and cold-hearted nation equated glory only with open splendour, unparalleled might and the magnificence of majesty, and had no concept of, or desire for, the quiet, dignified display of moral excellence and devotion to the will of His Father that belonged to the Lord in the days of His flesh.

Glory is the outward manifestation of qualities and attributes that are otherwise unseen. Every expression of the divine heart is glorious, and God (who alone is intrinsically glorious) thus displays His character in many different ways. Whether, and in what way, those manifestations of glory are perceived by men is determined by their condition of heart before God. The Psalmist says, "The heavens declare the glory of God; and the firmament sheweth his handywork" (Ps 19.1), and the believing heart exults in this display and gladly exclaims, "How great Thou art!". The response of the unregenerate heart, however, is solemnly recorded in Romans 1.23; "(they) changed the glory of the uncorruptible God into an image made like to corruptible man, and to birds, and fourfooted beasts, and creeping things". How can the glory of God be changed? Clearly, the intrinsic glory of the eternal God is totally unaffected by the wicked rebellion of men, but that which expresses His glory and would teach men of God and His ways is rejected, despised and polluted.

Glory seen in both Splendour and Lowliness

The first time we read of "the glory of the Lord" is in Exodus 16.6-7 where Israel murmured against the Lord because of their hunger: "And Moses and Aaron said unto all the children of Israel, At even, then ye shall know that the Lord hath brought you out from the land of Egypt: And in the morning, then ye shall see the glory of the Lord". As they looked toward the wilderness they saw the glory of the Lord in the cloud, "and in the morning the dew lay round about the host. And when the dew that lay was gone up, behold, upon the face of the wilderness there lay a small round thing, as small as the hoar frost on the ground. And when the children of Israel saw it, they said one to another, It is manna: for they wist not what it was. And Moses said unto them, This is the bread which the Lord hath given you to eat" (Ex 16.13-15). How wonderful were these two different displays of the glory of the Lord! We might say that in the one was the splendid demonstration of supreme power and awesome majesty, and in the other...? It would not be long before the people would loathe "this light bread" from heaven (Num 21.5) and count it a common thing, but was the "small round thing" not also a constant miraculous reminder of the supreme power and awesome majesty of their God? The cloud and the manna were both manifestations of divine glory, but human perception of them differed greatly. Was this not also true when the true Bread from Heaven graced this scene? The first mention of "the glory of the Lord" in the NT is in Luke 2.9: "And, lo, the angel of the Lord came upon them, and the glory of the Lord shone round about them: and they were sore afraid". The occasion, of course, was the incarnation of the Lord Jesus, and immediately we read, "And this shall be a sign unto you; Ye shall find the babe wrapped in swaddling clothes, lying in a manger" (Lk 2.12). Once again the shining glory of the Lord in the heavens gave way to a "small, round, white thing" lying upon the dew of the earth, and the true Bread from Heaven would reveal the glory of the Lord in a way never seen before. Initially, He "increased in wisdom and stature, and in favour with God and man" (Lk 2.52), but it was not long before the soul of the nation began to loathe Him. Nothing men could say or do would ever affect His intrinsic, personal, glory, but they took the "Lord of glory" and put Him to an open shame. How dearly men wished to deprive Him of His dignity and holy deportment, raining their blows and vile spittle upon Him! But, as the centurion watched the perfect Man upon the cross, and witnessed the manner in which He died, he was moved to say, "Truly this man was the Son of God" (Mk 15.39).

Glory Conferred by Another

As the Psalmist contemplates the smallness of man against the backdrop of the infinitude of God's creation, he says of man, "For thou hast made him a little lower than the angels, and hast crowned him with glory and honour. Thou madest him to have dominion over the works of thy hands; thou hast put all things under his feet" (Ps 8.5-6). Such was man's dignity and standing before the Fall. God made man to have dominion over all that He had made, and with that headship God conferred glory and honour upon Adam as well. The three things, glory, honour and dominion are linked. His exercise of dominion as a divinely appointed steward entitled Adam to be honoured by creation, and he, in turn, would both reveal the glory of God to creation and glorify God on behalf of the creation over which he had been appointed head. The various glories that God had given His creatures (1 Cor 15.39-41) would be directed and focused through Adam unto God. (The same principle of glory and headship is clearly taught in 1 Corinthians 11, of which we cannot speak now.) When Adam sinned, he not only lost his dominion by surrendering it to the Devil, but he himself came under the dominion of sin. All creation fell with him and became subject to suffering and shame instead of glory and honour. Hence we read in Romans 3.23 that "all have sinned [in Adam], and come short of the glory of God"; that is, all mankind and creation with him now lacks that glory that God intended him to display.

The Lord Jesus, the perfect Man and the last Adam, has won back that dominion by virtue of His sacrificial death at Calvary, His glorious resurrection and His ascension to the right hand of the Father. The Lord Jesus has taken humanity into Heaven and, as Man, has had glory heaped upon Him. Surely no fuller statement of the glory of Christ can be found than that recorded in His prayer in John 17. That God has conferred glory upon this Man is undoubted for He says, "Father, I will that they also, whom thou hast given me, be with me where I am; that they may behold my glory, *which thou hast given me*" (Jn 17.24), but, wonder of wonders, He also said, "And the glory which thou gavest me I have given them" (v.22). The Father has heaped glory upon His Son who, as Head of a new, redeemed, order of man has conferred that same glory upon those who are linked with Him by new birth! Thus we are to "the praise of his glory" now, and, very soon, "the Lord Jesus Christ...shall change our vile body, that it may be fashioned like unto his glorious body, according to the working whereby he is able even to subdue all things unto himself" (Phil 3.20, 21).